Creating your UCAS personal statement

Alan Bullock

One-stop Guide: Creating Your UCAS Personal Statement
This second edition published in 2011 by Trotman Education, an imprint of Trotman Publishing, a division of Crimson Publishing Ltd, Westminster House, Kew Road, Richmond, Surrey TW9 2ND

© Trotman Publishing 2011

Author: Alan Bullock

British Library Cataloguing in Publication Data
A catalogue record for this book is available from the British Library.

ISBN: 978-1-906041-56-4

Typeset by IDSUK (Data Connection) Ltd
Printed in the UK by Ashford Colour Press, Gosport, Hants

CONTENTS

ACKNOWLEDGEMENTS

I wish to thank the many university admissions officers who have shared their perceptions and advice, especially Mike Nicholson. Equally I want to thank Dave, Marianne, Gurpreet, Stephanie, Laura, Mark, Natasha, Rhodri, Kreena, Maria, Kim, Lorin, Andy and all the other students of Havant Sixth Form College who shared their experience of writing highly effective personal statements.

INTRODUCTION

The aim of this book is to help you to present your statement in the best possible way. It will give you ideas about what to write and advice on how to write it, but it won't give you a template or formula. That's because a good personal statement:

- focuses on the specific subject or courses you're applying for
- is personal to you in a way that makes you stand out from everyone else.

Or, in the words of one university admissions tutor (we'll call them 'selectors' for short):

> 'There is no such thing as a model statement ... each one should be different.'

So this book will show you how you can make your statement personal whilst also helping you decide what to include.

If you don't like writing about yourself or think you have nothing special to offer, then this book will give you confidence and reassurance and will help you find your unique selling point or 'USP'. If you feel confident about this already, read the book anyway. It will give you some extra ideas and you might find that what selectors are looking for is not what you thought.

Before we go any further, the most important advice of all is *don't leave it to the last minute*. It's best to give yourself several weeks to develop your statement, or at least several days, not just several hours. In fact, ideally, developing your personal statement should be an integral part of your research and planning, reflecting on what has led you to your chosen courses, why you are suited to them and what you want to achieve from them.

1. THE PURPOSE OF THE STATEMENT

Your personal statement should demonstrate to the selectors at your chosen universities that you're the kind of student they want to teach. The emphasis should be on why you want to study a particular course, not just a summary of your interests and achievements. You probably *will* write about your interests and achievements as part of your statement, but make sure they come across as being relevant to your application in some way, either directly or indirectly.

An increasing number of university courses are publishing their selection criteria in their prospectus, course booklets, web pages or UCAS Entry Profiles. So do seek out these resources because they will help you to decide what needs to be covered or demonstrated in your statement.

Make sure it sounds like you

Many applicants assume that selectors expect personal statements to be written in a very formal style. This is not necessarily true. They want to get a sense of the person you are and the way your mind works, so try and write it in a way that comes naturally to you and that sounds like you. Don't write things that you wouldn't say in real life, as it won't sound personal.

This can be a problem if you ask for help from a teacher, tutor, adviser or parent. It's sensible to seek their advice, but be careful if they try and rewrite it for you in their own words, because it may sound more like them than you. As one selector explained:

'If an adult has helped you to write it, we can tell.'

However, getting another person to double-check your spelling, punctuation and grammar thoroughly can be helpful – it's crucial that they are correct.

Don't be tempted to cheat by copying anything from the internet, from someone else's statement or from this or any other book. UCAS uses plagiarism-detection software to scrutinise every application.

2. TIPS FROM UNIVERSITIES

Each of these tips reflects advice given by selectors from various courses and universities. They're designed to give you a broad sense of what selectors are looking for. Some of the issues they raise will then be developed further in chapter 3.

The personal statement *is* important

Only a minority of courses hold interviews, so most selectors will base their decision purely on your UCAS application. Because of this, the statement is often the deciding factor. As one selector for a very popular English degree explained:

> *'When you've got 1,500 applicants for 75 places, then at the end of the day it's down to the personal statement.'*

Some courses that lead to professional qualifications may even use a marking policy when assessing your statement. One selector for nursing degrees said:

> *'We score the personal statement against our selection criteria and that's what decides if you get an interview.'*

Even if it's not considered so important, the statement may become vital at a later stage, as Dave found when he needed 300 UCAS points to get into his preferred university, but only achieved 260. He was still given a place, which illustrated another selector's tip that:

> 'The statement may become crucial if you don't quite get the grades we ask for, as we will then look at it closely before we decide whether or not to accept you.'

So, whichever way you look at it, it's highly important.

Demonstrate enthusiasm and individuality

The following tips from selectors are self-explanatory and build on the advice already given.

- 'What we really like is something that makes you stand out.'
- 'Most of all, we are looking for people who can demonstrate enthusiasm for the subject.'
- 'We're looking for people who are serious about studying and have a passion for their subject, but who also have a life.'
- 'A genuine interest in the course is the most important thing, but applicants can express this in many different ways.'
- 'Admissions tutors are busy, so you need to grab their attention. What is it that makes you different?'
- 'There are no rules for what to put in your statement, but a bit of originality, individuality and personality are very important.'
- 'We want to know what makes you tick.'

Or, as one mathematics selector put it:

'Tell me why you like maths and try to show that you're interested in the subject beyond the syllabus, like a book you've read or a maths club or challenge you've taken part in. I also like to hear about your outside interests because they show that you can think outside the box.'

A few selectors have also said:

'Demonstrate your passion for the subject, but try to do it without using the word "passion".'

Think carefully about structure and content

Here are some initial tips on how to construct your statement.

- *'Organise your material, structure it, don't waffle, give us an insight into your mind and sound interesting.'*
- *'Content is more important than style, but we don't object to a bit of style if the content is there.'*
- *'First impressions count; give us a picture of who you are; take time and care; edit it and don't try to cram everything in.'*

So, remember:

- structure is important
- be selective and don't waffle
- content is more important than style.

Again chapter 3 will examine this in more detail.

Tips on specific issues

The next few tips require no further explanation.

- *'If you're applying for deferred entry, explain your gap year plans.'*
- *'If you're dyslexic, don't hide it! Be open and honest. We won't count it against you and we're more likely to be able to provide for your needs. This applies to any special need or disability you might have.'*
- *'If you've had relevant work experience, we want to know what you learned from it.'*
- *'If you're applying for a joint or combined honours programme, talk about **both** subjects – and perhaps explain why this is a good combination for you.'*

But this one is more controversial.

'Avoid using quotations.'

Some selectors dislike quotations if you use them just for effect or to try and sound clever, for example by opening your statement with a quotation by your favourite writer, historian or economist. But, if a quotation is used to make a particular point in a reflective way, it might actually be effective. It goes back to the issue of content and style. In other words, don't use a quotation just to try and make you look good. It won't. However, it may be OK to use one if it helps you to explain an important point.

Another tip is:

> *'Don't be quirky – some admissions tutors like it but some don't, so it's risky.'*

Being 'quirky' could make you stand out as an individual, but possibly not in the right way. So do take care in the way you express your individuality. As another selector explained:

> *'We like you to be different, but not **too** different.'*

The same applies to the use of humour. A touch of humour can be very effective if it's part of your natural writing style, but on the other hand it can also be irritating. Again it's a matter of using **very** careful judgement. The next tip is a good one.

> *'Don't use lots of exclamation marks!'*

Don't use them as a way of trying to sound funny, because they won't and you will probably just sound flippant. Also:

> *'What you say in your personal statement is very likely to give interviewers an opportunity to form some of their questions.'*

If your course is one of the minority that hold interviews, then this is important advice. Make sure you keep a copy of your application and be ready to justify and elaborate on anything you say in your statement.

Balance your academic and extra-curricular interests

Consider these tips.

- *'We want to get a clear impression of the reasons why you want to study the subject and to see extra-curricular interests or achievements that show you are a well-rounded person.'*
- *'Do talk about your personal achievements because what you gain from wider university life is important.'*
- *'I like to see a 50/50 split between academic interests and personal interests.'*
- *'We want at least 70% academic interests and no more than 30% personal interests.'*
- *'Don't spend more than the last 20% of your statement on those extra-curricular activities and skills which make you a "rounded" person.'*

So it's clear that selectors are very concerned to see an appropriate balance between the curricular and the extra-curricular. But there are various views on what that balance should be, which again proves that there are no clear rules and that you should use careful judgement. Which should it be ... 50/50, 70/30, 80/20 or none of these? See chapter 3 for advice.

Show that you know what they want ... and that you've got it

A degree in aerospace engineering will require a different set of interests and qualities from a degree in American studies. So, to provide a focus for your statement, an important starting point is to research and identify the kind of interests and qualities that will be needed by your chosen course and then to:

'Tell us why you want to study the subject and demonstrate that you have some of the skills you need to be successful.'

How do you know what skills you need to be successful? Here are some suggestions.

- Refer to the Entry Profile that many university courses will have on the UCAS website and use your statement to demonstrate how you meet the given criteria. Entry Profiles vary in their usefulness, but some spell out exactly what's required.
- Explore universities' own websites, prospectuses, course booklets or other publications, as some of these will also tell you exactly what your chosen course is looking for.
- Go to some open days and ask!

Whatever you do, don't give the impression that you have an unrealistic perception about what the course, subject or profession involves. For example, sporting achievement isn't essential for physiotherapy or even PE teaching. That doesn't mean you should avoid mentioning sporting achievement in your statement but, if you include it, then consider why you think it's relevant. As one sports science selector said:

'All sport and no science will not impress.'

… or as one midwifery selector said:

'It's not about babies.'

For all courses, especially vocational ones such as midwifery or medicine, the skills, interests, achievements or experiences that you write about in your statement should all provide evidence that you've got what they want. The only way you'll know what they want is by researching it. So keep this in mind as we move on to chapter 3.

3. STATEMENT CONTENT

You have a maximum of 47 lines or 4,000 characters including spaces. So what do you include? Well, there are three factors that selectors tend to agree on:

1. What the selectors really want to know

What they want to know is: 'Why do you want to study our course and why should we select you?' So everything in your statement should relate in some way to this, either directly or indirectly.

2. Relate as much as you can to your chosen course

Some applicants don't focus enough on their academic interests. For many courses a 50/50 or 60/40 split would be about right, in other words at least 50% academic interests and no more than 50% personal interests. Some universities recommend that a 70/30 or 80/20 split would be best, especially if you are applying for a very academic subject. Even 90/10 or 100/0 would be acceptable if you feel that your super-curricular interests are more relevant than your extra-curricular interests (see p. 19 for a bit more on this). On the other hand extra-curricular interests show that you are a rounded person and can add impact to your statement, especially if you relate them back to the courses you're applying for.

3. Show what is unique about you

Selectors may have to read hundreds of statements, so try to make yours interesting. They want to get an insight into your mind, your personality and what you think (not just what you do). Be enthusiastic and try to include things that make you different from everyone else. Everyone is unique, so what's unique about you? What's your USP?

Collecting ideas and identifying your USP

You could start by making notes under different headings. If you wish, use some of the six headings on the following pages. Remember though, this is not a template for writing your statement, it's just a way of starting to collect ideas. So take note of the following.

- You don't have to use all six headings. For example, if you think your work experience is irrelevant or you haven't got any career plans, you don't have to write about them.
- They don't have to be in this order. Do it your way.
- If you can devise your own headings, all the better. You don't want your statement to have the same layout as everyone else who has read this book.
- If any of your five choices has a booklet, web page or UCAS Entry Profile that tells you what they're looking for, then take your headings from there instead.

Possible headings

1. Your motives for wanting to study the courses you have chosen

One way of doing this, but only if it's relevant to you, is to focus on what first inspired you. For example, was it an event, lesson, book, writer, teacher, place, visit, open day, holiday, talk, part-time job, project, work experience placement ...? If so, describe it and also mention anything that has subsequently reinforced or increased your interest (but if it was a film or TV programme, try not to choose one that hundreds of other applicants will write about).

Try to engage with the content of the courses you're applying for. What appeals to you about studying them at degree level? What topics or specialisms interest you and why?

If you're applying for a subject you already study, describe what you like about it. For example, you could write about particular issues, topics or assignments that have interested you or a field trip or project you've enjoyed. Or you could focus on specific books, writers, directors or theorists that have made an impact on you.

Then, if you can, try to go beyond your current syllabus and talk about your independent reading, personal interests, research or other insights into the subject. Selectors sometimes call these your *super-curricular interests* and they can help you to make a big impact in your statement.

If you're applying for something you haven't studied before, then it's essential to talk about your interest or background reading into the subject and to reflect on why you want to study it.

Otherwise just express your enthusiasm for the course or subject you have chosen, or express what appeals to you about the prospect of going to university in general.

2. Your criteria for selecting universities
It may be worth explaining if you've chosen them because:

- the courses are all modular or sandwich courses
- the balance of coursework and exams suits you
- the course content appeals to you
- they're all campus universities
- you want to stay at home or
- for another significant reason.

3. Your academic skills and qualities
Can you demonstrate some skills and qualities that are essential or desirable for your chosen course? If so, write about them in an interesting way or give actual examples as evidence, such as describing a specific situation where you demonstrated them.

Can you show how any of your school or college subjects, enrichment courses or learning support has helped you to gain confidence or learn good study skills, either in general or specific to your chosen course?

Can you show how you've taken responsibility for your own learning (an essential skill in higher education)?

Have you written an essay, extended essay or project that you were especially proud of, or made a valuable contribution to a group assignment?

Has there been a weakness or learning disability that you have striven to overcome whilst at school or college?

Have your current subjects combined especially well together?

4. Work experience, part-time job or other insights

If you've had relevant work experience or a relevant part-time job, talk about it and reflect on it. What skills or qualities have you learned or demonstrated? What have you observed? What have you learned from it? What has impressed you? What has surprised you? How has it changed your perceptions? How has it changed you?

If you can link it with your recent studies, such as explaining how your experience on a cardiac ward reinforced what you learned about the heart in AS biology, all the better.

If you've undertaken work experience or had a part-time job that isn't directly related to your chosen course, write about it if you feel it's saying something relevant about your skills and qualities. But if it doesn't add anything useful, leave it out.

Try to avoid bland comments such as *'dealing with customers has improved my communication skills'*. Instead be specific by describing a situation you've dealt with, how you cope with pressure, how you manage your time, why you work well in a team or how your communication skills have improved ... or something else that's relevant to your future studies or student life.

Be aware that Young Enterprise, volunteering, a conference you attended, a project that involved contact with an employer, a visit to the law courts, a production you took part in, an event you helped to run or an article you wrote, and so on, could be just as relevant as 'work experience' and could add real value to your statement, as long as you reflect on it.

Consider whether it's best to mention all your insights, or to focus in more detail on one or two. For example a dentistry selector might be more impressed by your observations on what you learned from watching one filling procedure rather than having a list of all the procedures you saw; and a drama selector will not be impressed by a list of parts you've played if you don't also convey a sense of what you want to gain from studying drama.

5. Extra-curricular interests
Do talk about your other interests, experiences, hobbies or achievements. They can demonstrate relevant skills, qualities or knowledge. They can also show that you're someone who will put a lot into (and get a lot out of) your time at university and that you can cope with academic study whilst also having a life.

If there's anything you've ever achieved that nobody else you know has achieved, or if you have a talent that you are proud of, write about it.

Don't just say that you like reading. If you do, be specific.

If your only interest is shopping, socialising or supporting Manchester United, leave it out because you will sound like hundreds of other applicants, unless you can say it in an interesting and academically relevant way. However, if the team you support is bottom of the West Midlands Regional League and you compile statistics for their website, this would be a brilliant USP. Even better, add a web link, giving the selector the opportunity to see your work.

> If you still can't think of a USP, maybe it's not too late to take up a new interest...

6. Career and/or gap year plans

Indicate your career plans if you want to, and if you feel it's relevant, but it's not essential.

If you're applying for deferred entry, or if you're in a gap year right now, explain why you're taking a gap year or what you are doing or hoping to do in it. Be honest. You don't have to be doing something relevant, unless you're applying for a course that demands it. But it would be good to say what you intend to gain from your gap year and to indicate how you intend to keep your reading or study skills active.

Now prioritise your material

Don't try to cram everything in. Be selective. Choose the points that you feel are most relevant or have the most impact.

Before you decide whether to include something, ask yourself '**SO WHAT?**' For example: *'In my spare time I play badminton.'* So what? Does it add something that's relevant to your application? If not, leave it out.

If your first draft is too long, then go through it in great detail and remove every single word that isn't totally necessary.

Some general tips on how to write it ... but don't copy any of the examples

Open with an interesting sentence that doesn't begin with 'I' and that doesn't include the words 'from a young age'

For example, explaining how the use of sustainable materials in the Welsh Assembly building first drew your attention to the relationship between design and the environment would be a more interesting opening than: *'I have wanted to be an architect from a young age.'*

Don't just say what you do, reflect on what you do

If you're applying for marketing, criminology or anthropology and want to mention your Saturday job in a clothes shop, then try to link your observations in an interesting way. For example, have you noticed how sales promotions influence customers or how different management styles impact on staff motivation or how customers or shoplifters show certain patterns of behaviour? Or have you learned some techniques for dealing with aggressive customers or persuading people to buy?

Don't state the obvious

When reflecting on what you gained from your work experience in an accounts firm, don't then waste space by saying *'... which is a useful skill for a degree in accountancy'*. They know it is. You don't have to spell it out. And don't waste space saying: *'I am studying A levels in maths, chemistry and biology'* as this is stated elsewhere in your application.

Ideally use paragraphs or headings

Using paragraphs or headings makes it easier to read and it will look more structured, especially if you leave a line between paragraphs. But this will also take up more space. It's good to make full use of your 47 lines, but it's also good to break up the text. You must choose for yourself. Most importantly, don't waffle or repeat yourself.

Hide your thesaurus

You won't impress selectors with pompous vocabulary that you wouldn't use in real life. If you wouldn't use it in conversation or discussion, don't put it in your statement as it may make you sound pretentious.

Ending the statement strongly

It's important to finish on a positive note but there are no rules. Marianne, a successful Cambridge applicant, used the 'necklace approach' where her ending linked back to her opening.

On the other hand some students waste several lines by ending with a paragraph that explains what they've said already, or with something cheesy about how their time at university is going to fuel them with desire and self-fulfilment.

If you really mean it, that's great, but if it's just said for effect, then don't do it. The worst thing to say is: *'As I've already said ...'*. If you've already said it, don't say it again.

WHAT IF YOU'RE APPLYING FOR A MIXTURE OF COURSES?

It's easier to write your statement if you've applied for the same course or subject in all five choices. However, if you're applying for a mixture of courses, put yourself in the position of each selector who will read it.

You could write one paragraph on each choice, but this could have the effect of putting them *all* off. A better approach might be to make all of your statement relevant in some way to all of your choices. If you can't manage this, then seek advice about whether your choices are wise.

If one of your choices is very different from the other four (such as if you're applying to four medical, dental or veterinary schools), it's advisable to focus your statement on the four. Then check whether the 'fifth choice' will consider you, even though your statement is focused on the others, or whether they might even be prepared to accept a separate statement emailed or posted to them. If they won't accept either, then choose something else as your fifth choice.

4. CASE STUDIES

These successful UCAS applicants illustrate how the advice in this book can be used well.

Examples of good USPs

Laura applied for psychology. She also worked part-time on a supermarket fish-counter. Totally irrelevant, you might think. But in her statement she compared the satisfaction she gained from knowing how to gut and fillet a mackerel with the satisfaction she gained from carrying out statistical analyses of experimental results in A level psychology. This met several of the entry criteria in one sentence and was a great USP and a superb example of how to apply the **'So what?'** factor.

Kim applied for music and took the risk of opening her statement with *'Hi, I'm Kim and I'm a tuba player.'* She was successful because the rest of her statement was excellent and because female tuba players are rare. So her USP was established in line one. Saying 'Hi' isn't recommended but, in Kim's case, she wanted to use an informal style and her USP and the general content of her statement were so good that it minimised the risk.

Highlighting things learnt from work experience

Mark applied for primary teaching and devoted the first 29 lines of his statement to a series of very interesting reflections on his work experience in a school and play-scheme.

Identifying the criteria to cover

Natasha applied for a mixture of courses in English language, linguistics and speech sciences. She used the relevant UCAS Entry Profiles and course websites to identify all the entry criteria and wrote them down in big 'speech bubbles'. She found that a lot of her academic and personal achievements tied in with the criteria and said *'it then became quite easy to write and it only took me one night to produce my first draft'*.

Rhodri applied for business studies. He used headings like those in chapter 3 to draw a spider diagram, with various offshoots branching out, and said *'from then it became fun and easy to do'*.

Giving the statement a personal touch

Kreena initially made the mistake of using posh vocabulary that she thought would really impress, but which didn't sound anything like her at all. She then rewrote it in her own personal style. As a result it was much more interesting and, as Kreena herself said, *'made me realise why my first draft sounded so fake'*.

Maria applied for film production and her statement vividly described her personal, academic and practical interests in film, literature and drama and then summarised what she looked forward to gaining from her university studies. She said: *'I made a list of headings and under each one I just kept writing what came naturally in a "stream of consciousness". It went way over the limit but then I hacked away at it and narrowed it down to what was most relevant, which actually took it below 47 lines. So then I embellished it, but I didn't use a thesaurus because I wanted it to sound like me'.*

Lorin applied for law. She only used nine lines to explain her interest in the subject, but she placed it into the context of how she arrived in Britain at the age of 13 and then reflected on her personal achievements and the challenges she has overcome. The qualities, skills and resilience that this demonstrated matched the selection criteria for her chosen courses and also made compelling reading. Lorin's advice is: *'Tell your story and add your own ingredients and your personal touch.'*

5. GETTING STARTED

As I said at the beginning, there is no such thing as a model statement and you may have noticed that this book hasn't included a single example of what a statement should look like. So where are *you* going to start?

Mike Nicholson from Oxford University has some good advice on this:

> *'It's hard when you're faced with a blank screen and 47 lines to write, so don't think about it in those terms. Either focus on the first paragraph OR write without trying to keep it to 4,000 characters. It's much easier to edit something that's too long than to aim for the right length in your first draft.'*

Many applicants also find it really helpful to list the entry criteria or a series of headings and then create bullet-points, spider diagrams or 'speech bubbles'.

Or imagine yourself having a coffee with the selectors and explaining to them:

- what has led you to your chosen courses
- why you are suited to them and enthusiastic about studying their course
- what you want them to help you achieve from the whole experience.

You may find it helpful to use a combination of these approaches but, whatever method you choose, if you know what you want to study, and you're in a positive frame of mind, then grab the moment and start drafting your statement. It's always best to work on it when you're feeling good about yourself.

You are unique. Everyone is. So demonstrate this in your statement.